50 Hidden Amazon Recipes

By: Kelly Johnson

Table of Contents

- Grilled Piranha with Citrus Marinade
- Amazonian Fire-Roasted Plantains
- Cassava Root Mash with Garlic Butter
- Jungle Pepper-Spiced Fish Stew
- Smoked Tambaqui Ribs with Tamarind Glaze
- Wild River Shrimp in Coconut Sauce
- Paca Stew with Roasted Peppers
- Exotic Guava-Glazed Chicken Skewers
- Pitanga Berry Chutney
- Rainforest Brazil Nut Pesto
- Smoked Pacu with Mango Salsa
- Spicy Tucupi Sauce with Grilled Cassava
- Papaya and Charred Pineapple Salad
- Açai Bowl with Amazonian Honey
- Amazonian Fire Pepper Hot Sauce
- Manioc Flatbread with Herb Butter
- Guaraná Energy Smoothie
- Rainforest Herb-Crusted River Fish
- Roasted Heart of Palm Salad
- Tamarillo Chili Sauce
- Cacao-Rubbed Venison Steaks
- Tapioca Crepes with Tropical Fruits
- Passionfruit-Infused Roasted Duck
- Jungle Lime and Ginger Tea
- Roasted Amazonian Nuts with Spices
- Coconut and Cashew Rice Pudding
- Spiced Amazonian Cornbread
- Amazonian Smoked Peppers Salsa
- Roasted Pineapple and Brazil Nut Cake
- Piranha Broth with Wild Herbs
- Wild Boar with Yuca and Peppers
- Starfruit and Papaya Chutney
- Fire-Grilled River Lobster with Citrus
- Jungle Honey-Glazed Plantain Chips
- Spiced Camu Camu Sorbet

- Grilled Catfish Wrapped in Banana Leaves
- Brazilian Nut and Chocolate Tart
- Cashew Fruit and Chili Jam
- Pirarucu Ceviche with Coconut Cream
- Smoked Turkey with Cupuaçu Sauce
- Charred Peppers with Rainforest Salsa
- Fire-Roasted Jungle Bananas
- Roasted Tapioca and Cheese Bread
- Wild Berry Infused Rice
- Spicy Amazonian Peppercorn Sauce
- Sweet Potato and Cassava Pancakes
- Papaya-Glazed Pork Belly
- Toasted Coconut and Açai Smoothie
- Jungle-Inspired Spiced Hot Chocolate
- Pineapple and Starfruit Sorbet

Grilled Piranha with Citrus Marinade

Ingredients:

- 2 whole piranhas, cleaned and scaled
- 2 limes, juiced
- 1 orange, juiced
- 3 cloves garlic, minced
- 1 tbsp olive oil
- 1 tsp salt
- ½ tsp black pepper
- ½ tsp paprika
- 1 tbsp chopped cilantro

Instructions:

1. In a bowl, mix lime juice, orange juice, garlic, olive oil, salt, pepper, and paprika.
2. Marinate the piranha in the mixture for at least 30 minutes.
3. Preheat the grill to medium heat.
4. Grill the fish for 5-7 minutes per side until the skin is crispy and the flesh flakes easily.
5. Garnish with cilantro and serve with rice or plantains.

Amazonian Fire-Roasted Plantains

Ingredients:

- 3 ripe plantains
- 1 tbsp coconut oil
- 1 tsp cinnamon
- 1 tbsp honey

Instructions:

1. Preheat a grill or open flame.
2. Slice plantains in half lengthwise.
3. Brush with coconut oil and sprinkle with cinnamon.
4. Grill for 3-5 minutes per side until caramelized.
5. Drizzle with honey before serving.

Cassava Root Mash with Garlic Butter

Ingredients:

- 2 lbs cassava root, peeled and chopped
- 3 tbsp butter
- 4 cloves garlic, minced
- ½ cup coconut milk
- Salt to taste
- Chopped parsley for garnish

Instructions:

1. Boil cassava in salted water for 20-25 minutes until tender.
2. Drain and mash with coconut milk and butter.
3. In a pan, sauté garlic in butter for 2 minutes, then mix into the cassava.
4. Season with salt and garnish with parsley.

Jungle Pepper-Spiced Fish Stew

Ingredients:

- 1 lb white fish (such as tambaqui or tilapia), cubed
- 1 tbsp coconut oil
- 1 onion, chopped
- 2 cloves garlic, minced
- 1 red bell pepper, diced
- 1 yellow bell pepper, diced
- 2 tomatoes, chopped
- 1 tsp cumin
- ½ tsp smoked paprika
- ½ tsp chili flakes
- 2 cups fish stock
- ½ cup coconut milk
- Salt and pepper to taste
- Fresh cilantro for garnish

Instructions:

1. Heat coconut oil in a pot over medium heat.
2. Sauté onion and garlic until fragrant.
3. Add bell peppers, tomatoes, and spices, cooking for 3 minutes.
4. Pour in fish stock and bring to a simmer.
5. Add the fish and coconut milk, cooking for 10 minutes.
6. Season with salt and pepper, garnish with cilantro, and serve.

Smoked Tambaqui Ribs with Tamarind Glaze

Ingredients:

- 2 lbs tambaqui ribs
- 1 tsp salt
- ½ tsp black pepper
- 1 tsp smoked paprika
- 1 tbsp olive oil

For the Tamarind Glaze:

- ¼ cup tamarind paste
- 2 tbsp honey
- 1 tbsp soy sauce
- 1 tbsp lime juice

Instructions:

1. Season tambaqui ribs with salt, pepper, paprika, and olive oil.
2. Smoke over low heat (225°F) for 2-3 hours.
3. Mix glaze ingredients and brush onto ribs.
4. Grill for 5 minutes, caramelizing the glaze.
5. Serve with roasted plantains or rice.

Wild River Shrimp in Coconut Sauce

Ingredients:

- 1 lb wild shrimp, peeled and deveined
- 1 tbsp coconut oil
- 1 onion, chopped
- 2 cloves garlic, minced
- 1 tbsp ginger, grated
- 1 tsp turmeric
- ½ tsp chili flakes
- 1 cup coconut milk
- Juice of 1 lime
- Salt and pepper to taste
- Fresh cilantro for garnish

Instructions:

1. Heat coconut oil in a pan over medium heat.
2. Sauté onion, garlic, and ginger until fragrant.
3. Add turmeric and chili flakes, stirring.
4. Pour in coconut milk and bring to a simmer.
5. Add shrimp and cook for 5 minutes until pink.
6. Season with lime juice, salt, and pepper. Garnish with cilantro.

Paca Stew with Roasted Peppers

Ingredients:

- 1 lb paca meat (or substitute with rabbit or pork)
- 2 tbsp olive oil
- 1 onion, chopped
- 3 cloves garlic, minced
- 2 roasted bell peppers, sliced
- 1 tsp cumin
- ½ tsp cayenne pepper
- 2 cups beef or vegetable broth
- 1 tomato, chopped
- Salt and pepper to taste
- Fresh parsley for garnish

Instructions:

1. Heat olive oil in a pot and brown the paca meat.
2. Remove meat and sauté onions and garlic.
3. Add roasted peppers, cumin, cayenne, and tomato.
4. Return the meat to the pot and pour in broth.
5. Simmer for 1 hour until meat is tender.
6. Season with salt and pepper, garnish with parsley, and serve.

Exotic Guava-Glazed Chicken Skewers

Ingredients:

- 1 lb chicken breast, cubed
- ½ cup guava paste
- 2 tbsp soy sauce
- 1 tbsp honey
- 1 tbsp lime juice
- 1 tsp garlic powder
- 1 tsp paprika
- Salt and pepper to taste
- Skewers

Instructions:

1. Mix guava paste, soy sauce, honey, lime juice, garlic powder, and paprika.
2. Marinate chicken in the mixture for 1 hour.
3. Thread chicken onto skewers.
4. Grill over medium heat for 10-12 minutes, turning occasionally.
5. Serve hot with fresh lime wedges.

Pitanga Berry Chutney

Ingredients:

- 1 cup pitanga berries (or substitute with cranberries)
- ¼ cup sugar
- 1 tbsp lime juice
- ½ tsp cinnamon
- ¼ tsp ginger powder
- Pinch of salt

Instructions:

1. In a saucepan, combine all ingredients over medium heat.
2. Simmer for 10-15 minutes until berries break down and thicken.
3. Remove from heat and cool before serving.
4. Use as a topping for meats, bread, or cheese.

Rainforest Brazil Nut Pesto

Ingredients:

- ½ cup Brazil nuts
- 2 cups fresh basil leaves
- 2 cloves garlic
- ½ cup grated Parmesan cheese
- ½ cup olive oil
- Juice of ½ lemon
- Salt and pepper to taste

Instructions:

1. Toast Brazil nuts in a dry pan for 2 minutes, then let them cool.
2. Blend nuts, basil, garlic, and Parmesan until coarse.
3. Slowly add olive oil while blending until smooth.
4. Mix in lemon juice, salt, and pepper.
5. Serve with pasta, grilled meats, or as a dip.

Smoked Pacu with Mango Salsa

Ingredients:

- 2 pacu fillets
- 1 tsp salt
- ½ tsp black pepper
- 1 tsp smoked paprika
- 1 tbsp olive oil
- Wood chips for smoking

For the Mango Salsa:

- 1 ripe mango, diced
- ½ red onion, minced
- 1 jalapeño, finely chopped
- Juice of 1 lime
- 2 tbsp chopped cilantro

Instructions:

1. Season pacu fillets with salt, pepper, paprika, and olive oil.
2. Set up a smoker or grill with wood chips and smoke fillets for 30 minutes.
3. Mix salsa ingredients and let sit for 10 minutes.
4. Serve smoked pacu with mango salsa on top.

Spicy Tucupi Sauce with Grilled Cassava

Ingredients:

- 1 cup tucupi sauce (fermented cassava broth)
- 1 tbsp olive oil
- 2 cloves garlic, minced
- ½ tsp chili flakes
- ½ tsp turmeric
- Salt to taste
- 2 cassava roots, peeled and sliced

Instructions:

1. Boil cassava in salted water for 15 minutes, then grill until golden.
2. In a pan, heat olive oil and sauté garlic.
3. Add tucupi sauce, chili flakes, and turmeric, simmering for 5 minutes.
4. Season with salt and drizzle over grilled cassava.

Papaya and Charred Pineapple Salad

Ingredients:

- 1 cup diced ripe papaya
- 1 cup pineapple slices
- 1 tbsp honey
- 1 tbsp lime juice
- ½ cup mixed greens
- ¼ cup toasted Brazil nuts

Instructions:

1. Grill pineapple slices until slightly charred.
2. Toss with papaya, honey, and lime juice.
3. Serve over mixed greens with Brazil nuts sprinkled on top.

Açai Bowl with Amazonian Honey

Ingredients:

- 1 frozen açai packet
- 1 banana
- ½ cup mixed berries
- ½ cup coconut milk
- 1 tbsp Amazonian honey
- Granola and coconut flakes for topping

Instructions:

1. Blend açai, banana, berries, and coconut milk until smooth.
2. Pour into a bowl and drizzle with honey.
3. Top with granola and coconut flakes.

Amazonian Fire Pepper Hot Sauce

Ingredients:

- 5 Amazonian fire peppers (or habaneros)
- 2 cloves garlic
- ½ cup vinegar
- 1 tbsp lime juice
- ½ tsp salt
- 1 tsp honey

Instructions:

1. Blend all ingredients until smooth.
2. Simmer on low heat for 10 minutes.
3. Cool and store in a jar for up to 2 weeks.

Manioc Flatbread with Herb Butter

Ingredients:

- 2 cups manioc flour
- ½ tsp salt
- 1 cup warm water
- 2 tbsp butter
- 1 tbsp chopped fresh herbs (parsley, basil, or cilantro)

Instructions:

1. Mix manioc flour and salt. Slowly add warm water until dough forms.
2. Roll into flatbreads and cook on a dry pan for 2 minutes per side.
3. Mix butter with herbs and spread over warm flatbreads.

Guaraná Energy Smoothie

Ingredients:

- 1 cup coconut water
- 1 tsp guaraná powder
- 1 banana
- ½ cup frozen berries
- 1 tsp honey

Instructions:

1. Blend all ingredients until smooth.
2. Serve immediately for an energy boost.

Rainforest Herb-Crusted River Fish

Ingredients:

- 2 river fish fillets (such as tambaqui or pirarucu)
- 1 tsp salt
- ½ tsp black pepper
- 1 tbsp olive oil
- 1 tbsp chopped fresh rainforest herbs (cilantro, basil, and oregano)

Instructions:

1. Coat fish fillets with salt, pepper, olive oil, and chopped herbs.
2. Sear in a hot pan for 4 minutes per side.
3. Serve with roasted vegetables or cassava mash.

Roasted Heart of Palm Salad

Ingredients:

- 1 cup sliced heart of palm
- 1 tbsp olive oil
- ½ tsp salt
- 1 cup mixed greens
- ½ avocado, sliced
- ¼ cup chopped Brazil nuts
- Juice of 1 lemon

Instructions:

1. Toss heart of palm with olive oil and salt, then roast at 400°F (200°C) for 10 minutes.
2. Mix with greens, avocado, and Brazil nuts.
3. Drizzle with lemon juice before serving.

Tamarillo Chili Sauce

Ingredients:

- 5 tamarillos, peeled and chopped
- 2 red chili peppers, chopped
- 2 cloves garlic, minced
- ½ cup vinegar
- 1 tbsp honey
- ½ tsp salt

Instructions:

1. Sauté garlic and chilies until fragrant.
2. Add tamarillos and cook for 5 minutes.
3. Blend mixture with vinegar, honey, and salt until smooth.
4. Simmer for 10 minutes, then store in a jar.

Cacao-Rubbed Venison Steaks

Ingredients:

- 2 venison steaks
- 1 tbsp cacao powder
- 1 tsp smoked paprika
- ½ tsp salt
- ½ tsp black pepper
- 1 tbsp olive oil

Instructions:

1. Rub steaks with cacao, paprika, salt, and pepper.
2. Let marinate for 20 minutes.
3. Sear in a hot pan for 3–4 minutes per side.
4. Rest for 5 minutes before serving.

Tapioca Crepes with Tropical Fruits

Ingredients:

- 1 cup tapioca flour
- ½ cup water
- ½ cup coconut milk
- ½ tsp salt
- 1 cup mixed tropical fruits (mango, papaya, banana)
- 1 tbsp honey

Instructions:

1. Mix tapioca flour, water, coconut milk, and salt into a batter.
2. Pour onto a hot non-stick pan and cook for 2 minutes per side.
3. Fill with tropical fruits and drizzle with honey.

Passion Fruit-Infused Roasted Duck

Ingredients:

- 1 whole duck
- ½ cup passionfruit juice
- 2 tbsp honey
- 1 tsp salt
- ½ tsp black pepper
- 1 tsp ground coriander

Instructions:

1. Rub duck with salt, pepper, and coriander.
2. Mix passionfruit juice and honey, then baste over duck.
3. Roast at 375°F (190°C) for 1.5 hours, basting every 30 minutes.

Jungle Lime and Ginger Tea

Ingredients:

- 2 cups water
- 1-inch piece ginger, sliced
- Juice of 2 jungle limes
- 1 tbsp honey

Instructions:

1. Boil water with ginger for 5 minutes.
2. Strain and mix in lime juice and honey.
3. Serve warm.

Roasted Amazonian Nuts with Spices

Ingredients:

- 1 cup Brazil nuts
- ½ tsp cayenne pepper
- ½ tsp smoked paprika
- ½ tsp salt
- 1 tbsp honey

Instructions:

1. Toss nuts with spices and honey.
2. Roast at 350°F (175°C) for 10 minutes.

Coconut and Cashew Rice Pudding

Ingredients:

- 1 cup cooked rice
- 1 cup coconut milk
- ¼ cup cashews
- 1 tbsp honey
- ½ tsp cinnamon

Instructions:

1. Simmer rice with coconut milk for 5 minutes.
2. Stir in cashews, honey, and cinnamon.
3. Serve warm or chilled.

Spiced Amazonian Cornbread

Ingredients:

- 1 cup cornmeal
- ½ cup cassava flour
- 1 tsp baking powder
- ½ tsp salt
- ½ tsp cinnamon
- ½ cup coconut milk
- 1 egg
- ¼ cup honey

Instructions:

1. Mix dry ingredients, then add wet ingredients.
2. Pour into a greased pan and bake at 375°F (190°C) for 20 minutes.

Amazonian Smoked Peppers Salsa

Ingredients:

- 3 smoked Amazonian peppers
- 1 tomato, diced
- ½ red onion, minced
- Juice of 1 lime
- ½ tsp salt

Instructions:

1. Blend all ingredients until chunky.
2. Let sit for 10 minutes before serving.

Roasted Pineapple and Brazil Nut Cake

Ingredients:

- 1 cup flour
- ½ cup sugar
- ½ tsp baking powder
- ½ tsp cinnamon
- 1 cup roasted pineapple, chopped
- ½ cup chopped Brazil nuts
- ½ cup coconut milk
- 1 egg

Instructions:

1. Mix dry ingredients, then add wet ingredients.
2. Fold in pineapple and Brazil nuts.
3. Bake at 350°F (175°C) for 25 minutes.

Piranha Broth with Wild Herbs

Ingredients:

- 2 whole piranhas, cleaned
- 1 onion, chopped
- 2 cloves garlic, minced
- 1 tomato, diced
- 4 cups water
- 1 tbsp wild Amazonian herbs (cilantro, parsley)
- Salt to taste

Instructions:

1. Sauté onion, garlic, and tomato in a pot.
2. Add water and piranhas, simmering for 30 minutes.
3. Strain the broth and season with herbs.

Wild Boar with Yuca and Peppers

Ingredients:

- 2 lbs wild boar, cut into chunks
- 2 cups yuca (cassava), peeled and cubed
- 1 red bell pepper, sliced
- 1 yellow bell pepper, sliced
- 1 onion, chopped
- 3 cloves garlic, minced
- 1 tsp smoked paprika
- ½ tsp cayenne pepper
- ½ tsp salt
- 2 tbsp olive oil
- 1 cup beef broth

Instructions:

1. Heat oil in a large pot and brown the wild boar on all sides.
2. Add onions, garlic, and spices, cooking until fragrant.
3. Stir in yuca and broth, then simmer for 1 hour.
4. Add peppers and cook for another 10 minutes.

Starfruit and Papaya Chutney

Ingredients:

- 2 starfruits, sliced
- 1 cup papaya, diced
- ½ cup onion, minced
- 1 tbsp grated ginger
- ¼ cup apple cider vinegar
- ¼ cup brown sugar
- ½ tsp salt
- ½ tsp chili flakes

Instructions:

1. Combine all ingredients in a saucepan over medium heat.
2. Simmer for 20 minutes, stirring occasionally.
3. Let cool and store in a jar.

Fire-Grilled River Lobster with Citrus

Ingredients:

- 4 river lobsters, cleaned
- Juice of 2 limes
- Juice of 1 orange
- 2 cloves garlic, minced
- 1 tbsp olive oil
- ½ tsp salt
- ½ tsp black pepper

Instructions:

1. Marinate lobsters in citrus juices, garlic, oil, salt, and pepper for 30 minutes.
2. Grill over an open flame for 4–5 minutes per side.
3. Serve with extra lime wedges.

Jungle Honey-Glazed Plantain Chips

Ingredients:

- 2 ripe plantains, sliced thin
- 2 tbsp jungle honey
- 1 tbsp coconut oil
- ½ tsp cinnamon
- ¼ tsp salt

Instructions:

1. Toss plantain slices with honey, oil, cinnamon, and salt.
2. Bake at 375°F (190°C) for 15–20 minutes, flipping halfway.

Spiced Camu Camu Sorbet

Ingredients:

- 1 cup camu camu puree
- ½ cup honey
- ½ tsp cinnamon
- 1 cup coconut milk
- 1 tbsp lime juice

Instructions:

1. Blend all ingredients until smooth.
2. Chill for 1 hour, then churn in an ice cream maker.
3. Freeze until firm.

Grilled Catfish Wrapped in Banana Leaves

Ingredients:

- 2 catfish fillets
- 2 banana leaves
- 2 cloves garlic, minced
- Juice of 1 lime
- ½ tsp salt
- ½ tsp ground cumin
- 1 tbsp olive oil

Instructions:

1. Rub catfish with garlic, lime juice, salt, and cumin.
2. Wrap each fillet in a banana leaf and secure with twine.
3. Grill for 10 minutes per side over medium heat.

Brazilian Nut and Chocolate Tart

Ingredients:

- 1 ½ cups crushed Brazil nuts
- 1 cup flour
- ½ cup butter, melted
- ½ cup sugar
- 1 cup dark chocolate, melted
- ½ cup coconut milk

Instructions:

1. Mix Brazil nuts, flour, butter, and sugar to form a crust.
2. Press into a tart pan and bake at 350°F (175°C) for 10 minutes.
3. Pour melted chocolate and coconut milk over the crust.
4. Chill until set.

Cashew Fruit and Chili Jam

Ingredients:

- 2 cups cashew fruit, chopped
- ½ cup sugar
- 1 tbsp apple cider vinegar
- ½ tsp chili flakes
- ½ tsp salt

Instructions:

1. Combine all ingredients in a saucepan and simmer for 20 minutes.
2. Blend slightly for a chunky texture.
3. Store in a jar and refrigerate.

Pirarucu Ceviche with Coconut Cream

Ingredients:

- 1 lb pirarucu fillet, diced
- Juice of 3 limes
- ½ cup coconut cream
- ½ red onion, sliced
- 1 chili pepper, chopped
- ½ tsp salt
- ¼ cup chopped cilantro

Instructions:

1. Marinate pirarucu in lime juice for 30 minutes.
2. Stir in coconut cream, onion, chili, salt, and cilantro.
3. Serve chilled.

Smoked Turkey with Cupuaçu Sauce

Ingredients:

- 1 whole turkey
- 2 tbsp smoked paprika
- 1 tbsp salt
- 1 tsp black pepper
- 1 cup cupuaçu pulp
- ½ cup honey
- ½ cup chicken broth

Instructions:

1. Rub turkey with smoked paprika, salt, and pepper.
2. Smoke at 225°F (107°C) for 4–6 hours.
3. Simmer cupuaçu pulp, honey, and broth for 10 minutes.
4. Serve sauce over sliced turkey.

Charred Peppers with Rainforest Salsa

Ingredients:

- 4 bell peppers (red, yellow, green, orange)
- 1 cup cherry tomatoes, chopped
- ½ cup red onion, diced
- 1 tbsp Amazonian honey
- 1 tbsp lime juice
- ½ tsp salt
- ½ tsp chili flakes
- 2 tbsp chopped cilantro

Instructions:

1. Roast peppers over an open flame or grill until charred, about 5 minutes per side.
2. Let cool, then slice into strips.
3. Mix tomatoes, onion, honey, lime juice, salt, chili flakes, and cilantro for salsa.
4. Serve over charred peppers.

Fire-Roasted Jungle Bananas

Ingredients:

- 4 ripe bananas, unpeeled
- 2 tbsp honey
- 1 tsp cinnamon
- ½ tsp nutmeg
- ¼ cup chopped Brazil nuts

Instructions:

1. Place whole bananas on a grill or open flame for 5–7 minutes, turning occasionally.
2. Split the bananas open and drizzle with honey, cinnamon, and nutmeg.
3. Sprinkle with chopped Brazil nuts and serve.

Roasted Tapioca and Cheese Bread (Pão de Queijo)

Ingredients:

- 2 cups tapioca flour
- 1 cup grated cheese (Parmesan or Brazilian Minas cheese)
- ½ cup milk
- ¼ cup butter, melted
- 1 egg
- ½ tsp salt

Instructions:

1. Preheat oven to 375°F (190°C).
2. Mix milk, butter, and salt in a saucepan and bring to a simmer.
3. Pour over tapioca flour and mix.
4. Add cheese and egg, mixing into a dough.
5. Roll into small balls and bake for 20 minutes.

Wild Berry Infused Rice

Ingredients:

- 1 cup jasmine rice
- 2 cups coconut milk
- ½ cup wild Amazonian berries (açaí, camu camu, or blueberries)
- 1 tbsp honey
- ½ tsp salt

Instructions:

1. Rinse rice and combine with coconut milk in a pot.
2. Bring to a boil, then simmer for 15 minutes.
3. Stir in wild berries, honey, and salt.
4. Let rest for 5 minutes before serving.

Spicy Amazonian Peppercorn Sauce

Ingredients:

- 2 tbsp Amazonian peppercorns (or black peppercorns)
- 1 tbsp butter
- ½ cup coconut milk
- 1 tbsp lime juice
- ½ tsp salt

Instructions:

1. Crush peppercorns and sauté in butter for 1 minute.
2. Stir in coconut milk, lime juice, and salt.
3. Simmer for 5 minutes and serve over meats or vegetables.

Sweet Potato and Cassava Pancakes

Ingredients:

- 1 cup mashed sweet potato
- ½ cup cassava flour
- 1 egg
- ½ cup coconut milk
- ½ tsp cinnamon
- 1 tbsp honey

Instructions:

1. Mix all ingredients into a batter.
2. Heat a pan and cook small pancakes for 2 minutes per side.
3. Serve with extra honey or fruit.

Papaya-Glazed Pork Belly

Ingredients:

- 1 lb pork belly
- 1 cup papaya puree
- 2 tbsp Amazonian honey
- 1 tbsp soy sauce
- ½ tsp chili flakes

Instructions:

1. Score the pork belly and bake at 350°F (175°C) for 1 hour.
2. Mix papaya, honey, soy sauce, and chili flakes for a glaze.
3. Brush over pork and bake another 15 minutes.

Toasted Coconut and Açai Smoothie

Ingredients:

- 1 cup frozen açaí puree
- ½ cup coconut milk
- 1 tbsp honey
- ¼ cup toasted coconut flakes

Instructions:

1. Blend açaí, coconut milk, and honey until smooth.
2. Pour into a glass and top with toasted coconut flakes.

Jungle-Inspired Spiced Hot Chocolate

Ingredients:

- 2 cups coconut milk
- 2 tbsp cacao powder
- 1 tbsp Amazonian honey
- ½ tsp cinnamon
- ¼ tsp cayenne pepper

Instructions:

1. Heat coconut milk and stir in cacao powder.
2. Add honey, cinnamon, and cayenne pepper.
3. Simmer for 5 minutes and serve hot.

Pineapple and Starfruit Sorbet

Ingredients:

- 2 cups pineapple chunks
- 1 starfruit, sliced
- ¼ cup honey
- 1 tbsp lime juice

Instructions:

1. Blend all ingredients until smooth.
2. Freeze for 3 hours, stirring occasionally.

www.ingramcontent.com/pod-product-compliance
Lightning Source LLC
LaVergne TN
LVHW081339060526
838201LV00055B/2733